The
DAWN

The DAWN

A Med Student's Roadmap to Finding A Light In Their Darkest Hour

Delicia M. Haynes, MD

purposely created
PUBLISHING

THE DAWN

Published by Purposely Created Publishing Group™

Copyright © 2019 Delicia M. Haynes

All rights reserved.

Printed in the United States of America

ISBN: 978-1-64484-018-4

Cover Image: Najah Gilreath of Photography by Najah

Hair Courtesy of Carmen Conaway

Makeup Courtesy of Barika Bridges

Back Cover Courtesy of Wyatt Peck Photography

Special discounts are available on bulk quantity purchases by book clubs, associations and special interest groups.
For details email: sales@publishyourgift.com or call (888) 949-6228.
For information log on to: www.PublishYourGift.com

I dedicate this book to Marilyn Haynes, who is and has always been the epitome of grace under fire. I am the product of the time you invested in me. I honor you for what you built when you thought no one was watching. Thank you for teaching me what resiliency looks like. Thank you for walking through fire to get me help. Most of all, thank you for being my mother. Heaven is a little sweeter because you're there. I love you.

TABLE OF CONTENTS

ACKNOWLEDGMENTS

Thank YOU! This book is a calling I've been running from for a long time. I would not have written this book without the love and support of my family, the friends who have become family, the coaches, teammates, and colleagues who have watched my form, known when to have my back and when to push me. Thank you to the teachers who intervened when my life was spiraling downward, to my Family First Health Center team, my patients who have put their trust in me, and the faith in God and the divine that was placed within me. Special thanks to the friends I've lost. May this labor of love be an enduring part of your legacy. I hope I've made you proud.

FOREWORDS

It is an honor and a privilege to support Dr. Delicia Haynes in her literary work. I first heard of Dr. Haynes when she decided to open a practice in our community at the conclusion of her residency in a local family medicine facility. Any medical community would welcome a physician with the talent and passion that Delicia has. I was really excited when she accepted our offer to join the clinical faculty at the Daytona Beach Regional Campus of The Florida State University College of Medicine as an assistant professor to teach and mentor our students. Praised as an excellent physician, teacher, and mentor, Dr. Haynes quickly became a very popular preceptor for our students. Little did we know about the journey that Dr. Haynes took to get to where she is now! It took the tragedy of the suicide of a student at FSU COM to open the door for Dr. Haynes to reach out and *really* mentor our students. Dr. Haynes offered to speak with them about depression and suicide as the national challenges that they are. Our students sat speechless as she shared her journey. Dr. Haynes shared her experience in the hopes of helping students become aware of, and educated about, the topics of depression and suicide amongst medical professionals. After every session that Delicia has taught, students have lined up to ask questions and thank her for reaching out to them. Delicia's message clearly resonates among medical students, residents, and practicing physicians. While there is no easy solution to the epidemic of depression and suicide in the profession of medicine, Dr. Haynes has offered one lifeline to help as she uses her experience to hopefully impact physicians and students in a positive manner. I hope that you enjoy and benefit from learning about Dr. Delicia Haynes and her passion to assist others as she shares her story with you.

— **Luckey Dunn, MD**, Florida State University College of Medicine Daytona Beach Regional Campus Dean

This book is written to get your attention and keep it! Dr. Haynes shares her personal history, her challenges and perspectives, and methods to prevent depression and suicidal ideations.

My son died by suicide as a 2nd Year Medical Student at the FSU College of Medicine in 2017. His depression was undiagnosed and untreated. His apparent feeling of hopelessness was unknown to anyone, neither his fellow students nor his parents. His suicide was a surprise to everyone; nobody saw it coming. He could have benefited from this book to help him realize he was depressed and needed help.

Depression and suicide amongst health professionals are at epidemic levels in our country. Dr. Haynes discusses her personal battle with depression and outlines how you can diagnose it in yourself and in your patients. She offers a lifeline to those in need. If you are suffering from depression, or think you might be, seek professional help.

As Dr. Haynes mentions, "Depression is a chemical flaw, not a character flaw and it can strike even those of great faith." Acknowledge your own humanity and take a "pause" if you need to. Recognize that YOU ARE NOT ALONE! Medical School Deans throughout the country are moving forward to stamp out the stigma associated with mental health issues and treatment.

Please learn from Dr. Haynes' passion and her experiences, to give you the tools for better physical and mental health, making you a smarter and better-informed medical professional!

— Col (USAF, Ret) Clayton Wittman, JD,
Father of Matt Wittman, former FSU College
of Medicine Student, Class of 2019.

TESTIMONIALS

"Dr. Delicia Haynes bravely shares her story of survival from depression and near suicide. She is an inspiring leader in physician mental health and has no doubt touched—even saved—the lives of countless medical students and physicians through her words. In this accessible book are simple solutions that can be implemented now to prevent the loss of our brothers and sisters in medicine. Since 2012, I've devoted my life to medical student and physician suicide prevention—a lonely crusade at times—so I am overjoyed that my friend Delicia has stepped forward to publicly claim her power and truth as a survivor. May medicine's wounded warriors heal through her wisdom. May her courage be contagious and lead to a day when all physicians fearlessly share their deepest struggles with the world, and most importantly, open their hearts to receive the care they so desperately deserve."

— Pamela Wible, MD, Author,
Physician Suicide Letters—Answered

"As a physician trained in adult psychiatry, I have spent my entire career helping individuals with depression. What has always struck me is that depression doesn't care who you are, as it can affect anyone. For those of us in the healthcare profession, we were often drawn to these specialties because of a desire to serve others and decrease suffering whenever we can. What I have witnessed over the years is that healthcare providers, including physicians and those in training, can sometimes do a poorer job of helping themselves. Whether it is due to stigma or believing they are stronger than depression, the results can be catastrophic. I am so proud of Dr. Haynes for sharing her story. As she describes in her book, there are effective treatments and resources. There is hope for a better day."

— **Todd R. Cheever, MD, Adult Psychiatry**

1

KNOW YOUR HISTORY.
CHOOSE YOUR FUTURE.

Senior Year.

On a late frigid Kentucky night in January 1996, alone with my thoughts, I rolled a handful of various colorful pills from palm to palm trying to keep my tears from dissolving them. I thought, "It would be better if I wasn't here." I cleaned my room, wrote a note to my parents that I loved them and it wasn't their fault. I wrote a message to my little sister, the only black girl in her entire 6th grade class, and told her that she was going to be fine without me. Then I sat in my closet, closed my puffy eyes, and lifted the pills to my lips.

Just then, my dog started barking incessantly. It was after midnight and she was making enough noise to wake the dead. I was moments away from becoming one of them. I left the pills and went to check on her.

It was about five months into my move from Maryland to Kentucky in my senior year of high school when I first penned the words, "It would be better if I wasn't here." If you had asked me if I was suicidal, I would have answered, "No." I didn't know what depression was, nor did I think of myself as suicidal. I didn't really want to kill myself, I just wanted the pain to end. I wanted the berating self-talk to stop. I simply wanted to go away and escape the pain of existing. Death seemed more peaceful than my tormented mind.

As an army brat, I was used to moving, so when we moved at the end of my junior year, after the initial shock, I was full of exuberance with all the things I was going to do. At my new school I joined a few organizations, made some friends and participated in several events, including a pageant where I performed Maya Angelou's "Phenomenal Woman." I was even on the homecoming court. But I started having difficulty going to sleep, was tired all the time, and snappy to my siblings. I had always been someone who was fairly positive and respectful. But my first period Advanced Placement Spanish teacher received a lot of my ire. I even stopped speaking to my parents. They put the fear of God in me from an early age, so even in the thick fog of depression I knew snapping at them was not an option. Eventually, I also began having problems in school. Although I had always had excellent reading comprehension, I noticed I was having difficulty retaining information. I simply couldn't focus. While speaking, I experienced difficulty with word choice and had this pervasive sadness that I couldn't shake. My decline wasn't quick; it was slow and insidious. I'd always been someone who took care of their personal hygiene, but even about this I began saying things like, "I took a shower yesterday."

I didn't know what I was experiencing but luckily for me, I had an AP English teacher, Mrs. Bowker, who did know. One of the things she had us do was keep a journal, and in this way she had a front row seat on my slow decline. Mrs. Bowker saw me coming into my transplant senior year full of ideas and things that I was going to do, and saw that excitement decline to the point that I started writing things like, "It would be better if I wasn't here."

Rather than just seeing and ignoring it, she actually took the time to intervene. She pulled me out of another teacher's class one day and met with me. As an experienced teacher, she had seen the signs of depression and passive suicidal ideation before. She asked if she could call my dad. He came down and the three of us met. In an attempt to be even more helpful, she gave me a book about cognitive behavioral therapy. I can't say that I was able to read it at the time, but the fact that she took the time to bring it to me left a deep impression. If only I could have loved myself the way others so easily could.

I have to take a minute to give my deepest appreciation to teachers like Mrs. Bowker. If it wasn't for a teacher, all the amazing experiences I've had since that time would never have happened. I would not be here. At the time, I couldn't see possibility. If there was a light at the end of the tunnel, I was convinced it was a succession of trains. My intellectually creative mind turned against me and took me to depths I didn't know were possible. I couldn't envision life getting better and those depressive thoughts had me believing the lie that the world would be a better place if I wasn't in it. As a result of the meeting between Mrs. Bowker and my father, my mom took me to see a family doctor and a psychologist. By the time I saw the psychologist, even basic movement required considerable effort and sapped me of all my energy, but I slowly began to improve. Prior to moving to Kentucky, I had run track in Maryland. I had always loved track but at that point I could take it or leave it. Track season came around and my dad, a former Olympian, encouraged me to try out for the team. I did, and my father later became the track coach, met all my friends, and would deftly demonstrate jumping drills after work in his three-piece suit.

With a combination of activity, engagement, counseling and meds, the depression gradually lifted. I still didn't really understand what it was, but at least I knew the disease by name. Depression.

2

A FLAW IN CHARACTER OR CHEMISTRY? WHAT IS DEPRESSION?

Depression is often referred to as the common cold of psychiatry. More than 300 million people are affected worldwide, and the economic impact of depression is estimated to cost more than $200 billion per year. In the United States, more than 3.1 million adolescents and over 16 million adults are diagnosed every year with at least one major depressive episode and it results in a loss of more than $36 billion per year due to absenteeism and presenteeism (being physically present at work but functioning suboptimally). That number doesn't account for the large number of people who never get a formal diagnosis. Some mental health experts estimate that over half of those with depression never get diagnosed. Although depression is a common condition, it is also extremely misunderstood. Depression is one of those terms that is used very casually in today's lexicon, but it is anything but a casual fling with a bad mood. It is a flaw in chemistry, not character.

Depression, otherwise known as major depressive disorder or clinical depression, is a common and serious mood disorder and is one of the greatest risk factors for suicide. According to the CDC, suicide rates are up 30 percent since 1999. Brain chemistry worsens the longer the depressive episode lasts, so early identification and treatment are important.

There is no single cause of depression. Causes may include biological reasons, including genetics and chemical neurotransmitters (the chemical messengers of the nervous system). Psychological factors may also be a cause, to include self-esteem, self-worth, and confidence. Spiritual factors and Social factors such as job, school, or family loss may play a role.[i] There are several factors that put people at higher risk. Trauma, especially childhood trauma, increases risk. Hormones, especially those involved in the expression and uptake of neurotransmitters, are involved. Genetics also play a role. People who are diagnosed with depression have a 3-5% chance of having a first degree relative with depression. In order for someone to be diagnosed with major depressive disorder they must meet certain criteria that have been present most days for at least two weeks—not one day, not one week, not one moment.

Screening is one of the best methods to detect depression early. There are lots of different screening tools available but I prefer using the Beck Depression Inventory, both for screening and to evaluate the effectiveness of treatment. It's a 21-question survey that you can complete by circling the responses that fit you in the moment and adding them up. It gives you a score that indicates levels of depression. Scores from 1-10 are considered normal, 11-16 indicates mild mod disturbance, 17-20 signifies borderline clinical depression, 21-30 is moderate depression, 31-40 is severe depression, and over 40 is considered extreme depression. The scale is helpful because depressive symptoms have a wide range and you don't have to wait until you are in the extremes to intervene. I like the ease of use of the Beck Depression Inventory because when you're dealing with depression, everything feels hard, and the Beck Depression Inventory is simple to take. It's something that I do for myself, and that I recommend to patients. I give out depression inventories with the same regularity that I give out blood pressure and blood glucose logs because mental illness can also be a chronic disease and needs to be managed. Just as with blood glucose or blood pressure, it's important to track your numbers.

Among adults, as of 2016, according to the National Institute of Mental Health, individuals aged 18-25 have the highest prevalence of depression and suicide is the second leading cause of death in 15-29 year olds. The majority of medical students are in their 20's and are great at memorizing symptoms of a disease for a test, but that doesn't mean they can recognize those symptoms in themselves or their colleagues. One of the things that medical students love to use when they're studying tons of information is a mnemonic. I too learned the mnemonic device for recognizing depression, SIG E CAPS.

When a physician writes a prescription, they write SIG, which means directions. The E Caps stands for energy capsules because people who are depressed lack energy. The diagnosis requires five of 9 signs and symptoms, one of which has to be either anhedonia or depressed mood, as indicated by either subjective report (e.g., feels sad, empty, hopeless) or observation made by others (e.g., appears tearful. Children and adolescents may show symptoms of irritable mood.)[ii]

The **S** stands for sleep. People who have depression may notice that they are sleeping more during the day, and also having early morning awakenings with the inability to return to sleep. People who have depression will either have hypersomnia, meaning they sleep a lot, or insomnia, meaning they can't sleep.

The **I** stands for interest. Depressed people generally experience a loss of interest in things that normally give pleasure, also known as Anhedonia. People who enjoy being sociable may become recluses. People who love the arts feel like they could take it or leave it. None of the things they were passionate about will do anything for them.

The **G** stands for guilt, which also can go along with feelings of worthlessness. People with depression devalue themselves and tend to blame themselves for things outside of their control.

The **E** stands for lack of energy, which is what usually brings most people to clinical attention. No matter how much sleep a depressed person gets, they are tired *all* the time and lack the energy to do things they used to do with barely a thought.

The **C** stands for cognition, including difficulty concentrating and indecisiveness. Those with depression may find it more difficult to think through equations, which obviously can be detrimental in a professional or scholastic environment. One of the reasons we will be making this book available as an audio is because people suffering with depression may find difficulty with reading comprehension, notice difficulty with word finding and word choice, or may simply feel mentally dull.

The **A** is for appetite. Sometimes it's a loss of appetite and the desire to care for yourself, but for some emotional eaters, it can bring an increase in eating comfort food, so it is really the change of appetite. This increase in eating, especially of comfort food, may lead to weight gain.

The **P** in SIG E CAPS is for psycho motor agitation or retardation. Individuals may show more agitation or anxious movements, such as pacing and fidgeting. Conversely, they may have what's called retardation, which is more lethargic, sloth-like movements. Joy has a posture and so does depression. Often people who are struggling with depression will keep their head down and hunch their shoulders in an effort to take up as little space as possible, as if they are trying to disappear.

The **S** stands for suicidal ideation, having preoccupation with death and thoughts of suicide or self-harm.

In order to be diagnosed with depression, these symptoms must cause impairment or distress in occupational, social, or other areas and cannot be the result of substance abuse or another medical condition. In addition to emotional problems, people often experience physical symptoms, such as chronic pain and digestive issues. When evaluating you, your doctor will listen to your symptoms and may order lab work to rule out issues such as low thyroid, anemia, and other conditions that could present with similar symptoms.

These depressive symptoms do not happen in just one day. Depression is not having a bad day or just being in a bad mood. It means having at least five of those nine symptoms, with one being depressed mood or loss of interest in pleasurable activities for most days of the week, for at least two weeks.

Sadness is a normal emotion that everyone experiences at some point in their life. It is usually caused by a specific circumstance like a break up, the death of a close loved one, financial stress, or losing a job. Unlike sadness, depression doesn't need a trigger. While there are life events that can increase one's risk of having a depressive episode, depression can occur even when everything seems outwardly fine.

Sadness may last for a few days, but you are still able to enjoy things that usually give you pleasure. Someone dealing with depression feels sad and hopeless about everything and nothing is pleasurable.

Few people who slide into a major depression will notice the early signs and distinguish the difference. Depression can occur without external circumstances. It can occur without stress, loss of relationship, or deaths in the family. That's the hard part. While all of those things can certainly increase your risk for an episode, by themselves, they are not the cause. Depression is a chronic disease that can worsen, so staying abreast of your mental health is important. Generally, by the time patients come to see me, they've known "something" was wrong for a long time or that they "haven't been themselves lately." Sometimes their life seems to be fine and they feel they have "everything they need and have no reason to feel this way." This is especially true of my patients who have a strong faith background. They feel guilty for being sad and not having an attitude of gratitude. However, depression is a chemical flaw, not a character flaw and it can strike even those of great faith.

Remembering the signs and symptoms of depression are helpful, but knowing that doesn't make you immune to it. Knowing the diagnosis of any disease doesn't make you immune to it, even after you put on a white coat.

Major Depressive Disorder has 9 symptoms. You need 5 of the 9, with one being depressed mood or anhedonia continuously for 2 weeks.

1. Depressed mood (frequent crying, mood swings).

2. Lack of interest.

3. Appetite changes, to include an excess in the intake of comfort foods, which can lead to weight gain, or lack of appetite, which can lead to weight loss.

4. Sleep change. Sleeping too much or too little.

5. Psychomotor activity, referring to activity of the mind and body, may be slow (psychomotor retardation) or anxious (psychomotor agitation). Depressed people tend to keep head and shoulders down and try to fit into the smallest space.

6. Loss of energy, feeling weak. Normal activities require lots of effort.

7. Guilt. Blaming self for any misfortune and feeling worthless, unliked, and unwanted; helpless and hopeless.

8. Concentration. Unable to complete daily activities.

9. Self-harm and suicidal thoughts.

3

KNOWLEDGE ISN'T IMMUNITY

When my second episode of major depression happened in my second year of medical school, I was pissed.

Following the episode in high school, I earned full athletic and academic scholarships to the University of Louisville. Vanderbilt had been my first choice, but I was offered only a partial scholarship there. My dad said he could mortgage the house to make up the difference, and not knowing what a mortgage really was, it sounded good to me. But my parents recommended I go where I would be paid to go to school. Several of my high school classmates were going to the University of Louisville, so I knew I would have community and that made me feel better about it. I loved college. I ran track, pledged my sorority, and sang in the choir.

After undergrad, I was blessed to be accepted to 3 of the 4 medical schools for which I applied. I was offered a full scholarship to the University of Louisville School of Medicine. They were considering a curriculum change and my class would have been the guinea pig. In contrast, the University of Kentucky had previously received a grant from the Robert Woods Johnson Foundation to reform their curriculum and had been in the newer model for a few years. The settled curriculum was appealing to me since no one at U of L knew the extent of the coming changes.

The University of Kentucky's Multicultural Affairs Office was run by Mrs. Anna Allen-Edwards, who went to my church, so I knew I'd have support there. I accepted my position at UK, and the multi 5-figure medical school education debt that came with it. Despite the debt, I've never regretted the decision. On some level, I knew the social support I would have through the Multicultural Affairs office was worth the money. Investing in one's mental health always pays off.

Although on paper I did well academically at the University of Kentucky, I could never say that I felt like I was excelling in medical school. It always seemed like we were all just a few steps from guaranteed failure at any moment. While most schools had switched to pass/fail, UK was graded, and I made A's and B's. But a few months into my second year, some of those familiar signs came back. I was having difficulty going to sleep. It was taking me longer to read and comprehend information. I spent hours on the same page of material I had once whizzed through without issue.

I became a student leader in multiple organizations and reached out to do even more external activities to fill a deepening sense of unworthiness. I became president of the local chapter of our Student National Medical Association (SNMA), and regional leader in the American Medical Student Medical Association (AMSA). I volunteered at a free health clinic and tutored at a local youth facility after school. I truly enjoyed all of these things, but when I'm honest with myself, I know I was trying to fill an internal void with an external source. While assisting others helped take the focus off of myself, self-worth is an inside game. I'm naturally a competitive person that loves to excel, but there is a distinct difference between being an achiever and having your intrinsic self-worth dependent on external accomplishments. Part of my self-worth was wrapped up in those grades, awards, accolades, and medals. I was always looking for my next carrot, even though I knew that self-worth is an internal matter.

I knew what depression was, so I was frustrated that it was affecting me again. It was a slow decline that at first, I thought was normal. By the time I faced the music that I was dealing with depression, I was furious with myself. "I know 'SIG E CAPS' cold, I should be immune!" I reasoned, as if knowing the histology of cancer would prevent a physician from succumbing to it. My father told me I needed to take a break. "This is med school. We don't take breaks," I responded. Pastor Gaines suggested I take a sabbatical. "This isn't a PhD program. We don't do sabbaticals," I told him.

Every day I got up, put on the mask, went to class, and absorbed absolutely nothing. I'd stare for hours at pages of information I'd usually speed through, unable to recall the previous sentence. I stopped participating in study groups. I knew I was in trouble and didn't want to take anyone else down with me. Over several months my grades declined. I had difficulty getting out of bed, lost my appetite, and couldn't sleep. When I had come to the point that I had to ask for additional time to take a test, the dean of students, who happened to be a psychiatrist, requested a meeting. He was the faculty advisor of one of the organizations I'd helped re-establish. The dean, like my high school AP English teacher, had a front row seat to my year-long decline during the time I served as President of the University of Kentucky chapter of the American Medical Student Association (AMSA). His words were measured; stern, but kind. He suggested I take a personal leave of absence while my grades were good and said it was still my decision to do so. The advice and wisdom coming from him made it possible for me to give myself permission to take a break. The House of Medicine's macho mentality doesn't usually afford this opportunity for a physician-in-training (or in practice) to acknowledge their own humanity.

Before I could heal anyone, I needed to be healed. Before I could serve anyone, I needed to take care of myself. The oath applied to me: first do no harm. Imagine that. We're human.

I took a break. Well, kind of. I reduced my medical school course load to one longitudinal ethics group course. I felt guilty about leaving my classmates and not being able to handle a full medical course load, but I enrolled in several undergraduate courses that medical students usually don't have time to take. Then, little by little I let go of the piano, pottery, and photography classes. The last class to go was weight lifting. I finally stopped when the guy I had been paired with based on the amount we lifted, didn't show up for class. A few months into my break, I was thrown into the middle of a perfect storm, facing five family deaths, from my grandfather to my three-month old niece. When others heard the story of me taking a break from medical school, they put my family tragedies in front of the depression, and I didn't correct them. It made more sense in that order. I had to have a reason, right?

I returned to medical school shortly after my three-month old niece Ayanna's funeral and did well. I even spearheaded a region-wide AMSA project, aptly titled "Physician Heal Thyself. Region 7 – A Region of Wellness", and an SNMA Region X Conference, "Combating Health Disparities: Education for Action. Promoting and Maintaining the Pipeline."

Despite taking the personal leave of absence, at graduation, I was awarded the D. Kay Clawson Award "for demonstrating personal qualities of both a scientific and caring physician, academic superiority, improving the academic environment of the college, and statesmanship as a student leader." I came into medical school thinking I would go into psychiatry, but I realized the people I wanted to serve were people who didn't realize they needed a psychiatrist. I also enjoyed preventive health and taking care of a wide variety of people and problems. I graduated and headed off to my first choice family medicine residency. Taking that break was the best decision of my career.

For those of us in involved in the education of medical students and residents, we are in a unique situation to distinguish when a student is having academic difficulty that stems from unaddressed mental health issues. If a student has been doing well through rigorous coursework in their first year and later starts to decline in their second, it's unlikely a simple academic issue. I thought I was alone but I was not.

4

YOU ARE NOT ALONE

During my second year at Halifax Health's Family and Sports Medicine residency program, we were required to give a grand rounds presentation, an hour-long academic lecture on a topic in front of physician peers. I decided to do mine on suicide and depression amongst physicians. The grand rounds faculty advisor was not on board with my topic and preferred I present on sleep disorders, which had been my first thought, but my insomnia was cured when I started reading about sleep. As I researched about suicide and depression in preparation for my grand rounds, I realized that I was not alone.

In preparation for my presentation, I researched and read the stories of several physicians like Susan, a 27-year-old married intern who had depression during medical school and had, in previous episodes, responded well to psychotherapy and medication. Like many doctors, she had perfectionistic standards and harsh self-criticism. Months into her residency program, she began to have depression again. She feared a lack of confidentiality if she used her insurance, so she didn't seek treatment. She was also afraid of the impact of psychiatric treatment on her ability get a medical license, so she waited three months before she began treatment. By then, she was unable to sleep and concentrate. She began treatment for depression just three weeks before her death.

I also read about Thomas, who was a married, 40-year-old child psychiatrist, and the father of three. He trained at prestigious universities and had a long history of poor self-esteem and insecurity. He began to have depression after his fellowship year. He was dissatisfied with his career and was contemplating a career change. He had become increasingly irritable and withdrawn and attempted to relieve those symptoms with alcohol. He would treat himself with anti-depressant samples available at his clinic and was in treatment with a psychoanalyst at the time of his death.

Many physicians neglect to seek help for depression themselves or to diagnose it in their patients. 40 to 60% of major depressive episodes go unrecognized. People with depression often start to think about death and even suicide, all the while not recognizing it as or calling it depression. Instead, it is more likely referred to as "burnout." Leading mental health professionals consider burnout a form of depression, but for those who are depressed, depressive symptoms are often attributed to other external challenges like marital and family conflict.

Sometimes depression is characterized by absenteeism from work, poor school performance, social withdrawal, loss of the sense of humor, and lack of motivation. Many physicians will postpone evaluation because they believe they are experiencing a normal reaction to the stress of training, but this is so often not the case. When I speak at medical schools now, I encourage everyone take an anonymous Beck Depression Inventory. The students are always surprised at their scores, because what they thought was just a normal, "This is medical school, my life is supposed to suck" mentality is actually revealed to be depression.

So, even though physicians and physicians-in-training know how to diagnose depression, having the self-awareness to be able to pick it up in ourselves and our colleagues is another thing. One of the reasons it's so important to treat depression is because approximately 15% of individuals with severe major depressive disorder will die by suicide, according to the text of clinical psychiatry. Every year, more than 400 physicians die by suicide. Researchers feel that number is under reported because sometimes the causes of death are reported as other modes of death in effort to help the families or because it's unclear. It would take the equivalent of an entire medical school to replace the number of physicians who kill themselves every year. The average doctor cares for approximately 2000 to 3000 patients. This means that when 400 doctors suddenly kill themselves, more than one million Americans lose their personal physicians. This happens every single year.

Attention to depressed and suicidal physicians is long overdue. As far back as 1858, John Churchill wrote in the Manual of Psychological Medicine, that physicians in England observed that a higher suicide rate exists among physicians than the general population. Since the 1960s, smoking related mortality among physicians has decreased by 60%. Between 1963 and 1991, deaths among physicians from cancer, heart disease, and other ailments dropped between 40 and 60%.[iii] Yet compared to the general population, physicians are at a higher risk for suicide. A 1999 study suggests depression is as common in physicians as in the general population. Male physicians have a lifetime depression prevalence of 12.8%. Female physicians have a lifetime depression prevalence of 19.5%. About 1.5% of those women will die by suicide.[iv]

If you compare that to the general population, the prevalence of depression for males in the general population is anywhere between 5 and 12%. The prevalence of depression amongst females is between 10 and 25%. *Wellner, et al.* in the 1975 Archives of General Psychiatry interviewed female professionals for a lifetime history of depression and found that 51% of female physicians had a lifetime history of depression. Amongst physicians, psychiatrists have the highest rate with 73% compared to 46% for other physicians.

Some of the studies on physician suicide are limited because of methodological flaws, as depression studies tend to largely rely on self-reported diagnoses rather than clinical interviews or validated questionnaires. Small study sizes in homogeneous populations are an issue, as well as publication biases and a general under reporting of suicides in the official statistics. Dr. Eva Schernhammer, MD, DPH, Assistant Professor of Medicine and Epidemiology at Harvard Medical School and adjunct medical faculty at the Medical University of Vienna, conducted one of the first meta-analyses of available studies on suicide rates among physicians. It was published in the American Journal of Psychiatry in 2004 and is called "Suicide Rates Among Physicians: A Quantitative and Gender Assessment Meta-Analysis". It was a meta-analysis of 25 international studies from 1966 through July 2003, which met quality standards for inclusion criteria.

In the study, Dr. Schernhammer evaluated for publication bias and calculated the rate ratio for male and female physicians, which was the suicide mortality rate amongst physicians compared against the suicide and mortality rate of the general population during the time period of the study. She evaluated for publication bias and the Egger test showed no significant evidence for bias in the data from studies on male physician suicide, but the data on female physicians shows some asymmetry reflecting a relative scarcity of studies with large numbers.

The combined result of the 25 international studies from *Schernhammer, et al.* suggested that the suicide rate among male doctors is 40% higher than general population and the rate among female doctors is 130% higher than women in general.[v] Another study, *Frank, et al.* published in 2000, cited a suicide rate 70% higher for male physicians versus the general population including other professions, and between 250 to 400% higher for female physicians than the suicide rate for others.[vi] This is important, because we know that women in the general population attempt suicide more often than men. Suicide rates for female physicians are about four times that of women in the general population. In the general population, the male suicide rate is four times the female suicide rate, but when we look at physicians, the rates of suicide for male and female physicians are roughly equal.

A women physician's health study in 1999 published that there are fewer uncompleted suicide attempts among physicians. The ratio of uncompleted suicides is 10 to 1, as compared to completed suicides amongst women in the general public, which is 15 to 1. When a female physician decides to end her life, she's more likely to use more fatal means. Since 1950, the number of female graduates going into medicine has increased nine-fold.

In 1975, Everson and Fraumeni determined that suicide was the leading cause of death for medical students and young physicians. This was later supported by a study by *Samkoff, et al.* in 1995, which found that 26% of deaths were due to suicide. The anonymous Beck Depression Inventories I collect from presentations to medical students consistently show a 30% rate of depression. Bottom line, if you are a physician or medical student who is experiencing depression, **you are not alone.**

5

RISK FACTORS

Contrary to what some may believe, suicide often takes the best and brightest amongst us.

Jonathan Drummond-Webb, MD
Aug. 29, 1959 – Dec 26, 2004

Dr. Drummond-Webb was the chief of pediatric and congenital cardiac surgery at Arkansas Children's Hospital and the first endowed chair of pediatric and congenital cardiac surgery. He performed the first successful implant of the DeBakey child ventricular assist device. He was featured in the ABC 2002 Documentary "ICU: Arkansas Children's Hospital." Dr. Drummond-Webb performed 830 surgeries in 18 months with a 2% mortality rate. He had been diagnosed with a rare tissue cancer on his hip in 2001 but was successfully treated with surgery.

"I work on very hard facts and very hard statistics," he said. "Even though we are driven by compassion, I think it's foolhardy to just proceed with compassion and heart alone...

The bottom line is that we're dealing with hard scientific evidence, and what I do demands ultimate perfection. I live my life wondering about the ones who don't make it. This is a high-risk business. We see children walking out; we also see children who do not make it."

Following Dr. Drummond-Webb's death, a colleague remarked, "Some would say they saved 98 out of 100. He [Drummond-Webb] looked at it and said 'I lost two out of 100.'"

According to a 1973 paper in the Journal of Diseases of the Nervous System, "Suicide Among Physicians: A psychological Study", "The definition of a high-risk physician is one who has struggled with depression, has problems with alcohol and drugs, has access to means, is driven, competitive, compulsive with excessive risk-taking, individualistic, ambitious, age greater than 45 in women and greater than 50 in men, graduate of a highly prestigious school, a physician who has a nonthreatening, but annoying physical illnesses, self-destructive tendencies, a guilty self-concept, change in status, a threat to autonomy or financial instability."

Having a support system and good relationships play an important role in mental health maintenance. In a world of increased social media, social isolation is high. Amongst professionals, social isolation and disturbances of beneficial social networks is common. The culture of self-reliance and lack of connectedness to extended family and community adds to the loneliness. Being single and not having children are linked to an increased risk of suicide. More female than male physicians are single or childless. Stress and burnout may be risk factors for all physicians, and female doctors may be subject to a double burden of being vulnerable to pressures of both family and work life.[v]

Compulsive personality traits, which are widely heralded as the key for professional success, may lead to more distant relationships. Divorce rates among physicians are 10% to 20% higher than the general population. Couples, including physicians who remain married, report more unhappy marriages, according to Medical Marriage 1996 by Wayne M. and Mary O. Sotile.

Physicians become masters of delayed gratification. Medical students spend years coping with the level of demand medicine requires, with the expectation, that later they will be rewarded with a happy, more balanced life. That doesn't always happen. Some of the risk factors for suicide correspond with risk factors in the general population, such as being divorced or currently having a marital disruption, being widowed, or never married.

The major risk factors were mental disorders and substance abuse disorders. More than 90% of those who die by suicide have at least one of these disorders: major depression disorder, bipolar disorder, and/or alcohol abuse.

In 1980, a study was done retrospectively, through interviews with family and friends, by the American Medical Association, and found that more than one-third of physicians who die by suicide were believed to have had a drug problem at some point in their lives, as opposed to, 14% in the general population. 42% had been seeing a mental health professional at the time of their death, as opposed to 7% of controls in general population. One-third had a history of at least one psychiatric hospitalization. There was a slightly higher incidence of suicide amongst their own parents, and they reported more emotional problems before age 18, than control groups.

It's estimated that 40% of physician suicides are associated with alcoholism and 20% with drug abuse. Prevalence rates vary, but data suggests that abuse of alcohol and illicit drugs by physicians is similar to the general population. Female physicians have a higher frequency of alcoholism versus the general population, according to the study by Bonk, at the University of Cologne Medical School of Germany. A few of my classmates became high-functioning alcoholics as their way of coping and numbing themselves to the stress and trauma inherent to our medical training.

Physicians are at increased risk for prescription drug abuse. Anesthesiologists are over represented among Florida physicians with substance abuse problems. They represent 5.6% of total licensed physicians, but 25% of physicians with substance abuse disorders. Some of the reasons are related to access and unintended secondhand environmental exposure.

There are special substance abuse programs for physicians all over the United States and Canada. Many of them are excellent, but some have come under fire due to conflicts of interests from referring impaired physicians only to facilities where its members had a financial stake.

6

BARRIERS TO TREATMENT

Barriers to treatment include both physician personality characteristics and very real concerns about the consequences of seeking treatment. Physicians have a need for control, which makes it difficult to accept a patient role and to ask others, perhaps especially other physicians who are colleagues, for help. Many physicians are wounded healers. Our personal experience with loss, abuse, trauma, and family conflict, attracted us to a helping profession.

The culture of medicine in the book, *A Doctor's Story of Friendship and Loss* by Abraham Verghese says, "There's a silent but terrible collusion, to cover up pain, to cover up depression. There is a fear of blushing, a machismo that destroys us." That macho mentality, always be strong and support others, is part of the problem when it comes to physicians seeking help. 35% of physicians do not have a regular source of healthcare themselves, according to the Archives of Internal Medicine, 2000 report, and physicians also tend to self-prescribe. The expectations in the culture of medicine are also a problem. George S. Kaufman once wrote, "The kind of doctor I want, is one who, when he's not examining me, is home studying medicine." And while obviously that would lead to a professionally astute physician, it definitely doesn't lead to a well-balanced life.

The culture of medicine requires or encourages perfectionism and workaholic standards. Physicians are humans and humans make mistakes. Mistakes in medicine can lead to catastrophic outcomes that have profound effects on both patients and physicians. There's an expectation to be available, that may lead to a sense of obligation that makes it difficult to set appropriate limits without great guilt. Setting time limits is often perceived as lacking in professional commitment. Our practice settings reward long hours and also reward self-neglect. Physicians in training are pushed to endure chronic sleep deprivation, which can lead to cognitive impairment and emotional fragility, taking on more and more work without complaint. They are pushed to distance themselves from patients and compartmentalize their feelings. All this enhances the development of a defense mechanism that makes it even more difficult to ask for help.

Another barrier is the VIP treatment that physicians often get when they're being treated by other physicians. Doctors often enjoy a special treatment with fellow physicians, and the treating physicians may be less aggressive in their treatment. Being a "VIP" may increase a physician's own sense of shame and stigma. In a study by Feuerlein, "Suicide and Attempted Suicides, Mental Health Professionals Treating Physicians," among suicidal physicians who sought help, over 50%, who later committed suicide, had been diagnosed with psychiatric conditions, but were not hospitalized before death. Mental health professionals treating physicians must treat them as a patient who just happens to be a physician.

There's also the question of confidentiality. Electronic health records make it easier for treating and non-treating colleagues to gain access to a patient's medical record. When that patient is a physician, there is an increased concern of privacy.

Depression is a common occurrence during medical training. In a study of nearly 200 medical students by Givens and Tjia in Academic Medicine 2002, only 22% of those who screen positive for depression actually use mental health services, and only 42% of depressed students with suicidal ideation receive treatment. Some of the barriers to getting treatment during medical training is lack of time (48%) and lack of confidentiality (37%). Student health plans usually require care in the setting in which they are educated, so students would have to go to a location where they might see some of their colleagues rotating through. There's also a concern that the person they would be seeing might at some point, actually be grading them, or in some way, involved in the advancement of their career. Other treatment barriers included stigma (30%), cost (28%), fear of documentation on the academic record (24%), and fear of unwanted intervention

(26%). Although there are several highly effective treatments for depression, many medical students are suffering in silence. By acknowledging our risks, we can decrease the stigma of mental illness in medicine.

One study in the Journal of Medical Education, "Effect of Psychological Counseling on Selection of Applicants for Residencies"[vii] by Oppenheimer found that residency prospects were reduced for students, otherwise qualified, with a history of psychological counseling. Rates of clinical depression among interns have been reported to be anywhere between 27 to 30%, and 25% of interns reported suicidal ideation.

The barriers to seeking help are often punitive, including discrimination in medical licensing, hospital privileges, and professional advancement. Practices of state licensing boards is another barrier.[viii] Physicians may try to hide their condition in order to protect their careers. Some state boards conduct investigations of physicians who seek psychiatric treatment, which may lead to sanctioning, regardless of whether there is any evidence of impaired functioning.

There are concerns that malpractice insurance, disability insurance, and hospital policies aimed at protecting patients may discourage physicians from seeking help by inappropriately identifying impaired physicians, focusing more on psychiatric diagnosis, and not actual incapability. In regard to licensing boards, in The Journal of the American

Medical Association, an article titled, "A Piece of My Mind, a Challenge to Licensing Boards: The Stigma of Mental Illness," printed in 1998, Steven H. Miles, MD drew attention to the discriminatory practices of his state's licensing board. The board required submission of psychiatric records solely based on his bipolar diagnosis, rather than on impaired professional abilities. The board justified their inquiry, saying that it was for the protection of the public. Miles refused access, arguing that he was in effective treatment and was not impaired. He said that impairment cannot be inferred from diagnosis alone and that, "Such policies deter physicians from seeking help, thereby posing greater risks to patient care from physicians' untreated illness." After a two year standoff, the licensing board changed its policy to focus on impairment, rather than diagnosis alone.

As early as 1983, the American Psychiatric Association expressed concerns about the discriminatory nature of questions on board licensure applications. Most, but certainly not all, state licensing boards have moved from questions about diagnosis alone, or treatment, toward questions about impaired professional performance at initial licensure and renewals, but for the Florida Board of Medicine, such was not the case at my initial licensure. Question 45 made no such distinction, and asked, "In the last five years, have you been treated for, or had a recurrence of a diagnosed mental disorder or impairment?" lumping both diagnosis and impairment together. An affirmative answer would result in requests for psychiatric medical records, as was my experience. When I filled out my initial licensure for the state of Florida, I froze when I came across the question. I took the form to the dean of students because at that time, the question was longer and lumped even more psychiatric diagnoses into one question. I only identified with one small word, so why would I check the "yes" box to everything. The dean did not agree with the questions but let me know I would be expected to answer in the affirmative. He also let me know that if I checked "yes", there would be requests made for my chart. I checked "no". Years later, preparing for my Florida licensure renewal, I came across similar questions. By now I had dedicated myself to learning more about depression and felt empowered. This time I checked "yes", and within 72 hours the phone rang and a board representative asked for my records even though I had no impairment. Luckily for me, I had been treated most effectively by my spiritual leader who had additional background in counseling. Now I am an advocate for making sure the medical licensure mental health questions focus on impairment rather than diagnosis. Creating an environment where physicians can get help protects the public. At the April 2018 conference of the Federation of State Medical Boards (FSMB), the board voted unanimously to adopt all thirty-five recommendations from the report of the workgroup on physician wellness and burnout. The first recommendation was that it is not helpful to ask questions about mental health diagnosis and that asking prevents physicians from getting treatment.[ix] Since the FSMB vote, several states have amended their mental health questions. If your state is one of the thirty-eight states that still asks doctors about their mental health when applying for a medical license, bring it to their attention that these questions may not be in line with the Americans with Disabilities Act. The function of the state medical boards is to protect the public. Removing barriers to treatment improves physician health, which protects the public. Illness is not impairment.

7

SUICIDE PREVENTION AND GETTING HELP

While no one can control the actions of another person, suicidality is both treatable and preventable through better detection of stress and depression. There is a window of opportunity to prevent suicide. Most people are symptomatic for several years before their death. Pharmacotherapy to treat depression is effective in over 70% of patients, but may require four to six weeks for effect, with treatment lasting at least six months. Medications such as Bupropion, a norepinephrine-dopamine reuptake inhibitor (NDRI), can be very effective for depression characterized by psychomotor retardation or inertia. Selective serotonin reuptake inhibitors (SSRI's) can be effective for people who have more anxious symptoms.

Electroconvulsive therapy (ECT) has been found safe and highly effective for refractory or catatonic depression. Transcranial magnetic stimulation (TMS) is a treatment that has also shown considerable promise. Psychotherapy combined with antidepressants is more effective than either alone, especially cognitive behavioral therapy monthly, for 10 to 16 sessions. The bottom line is, there are several effective treatments for depression, and if one doesn't work, keep trying. Complementary and alternative medicine may be effective for some people for preventing the return of depressive symptoms. We'll dive more into that in the next chapter. Medications may be effective for biological and chemical factors, while talk therapy may be effective for psychological and social factors. No one treatment is right for everyone, so keep trying until you find which strategy or combination works for you.

For prevention, we can recognize depression and suicidality in our patients, our students, our colleagues, and ourselves. Some of those warning signs include a decline in job performance, high rates of absenteeism, being noticeably more withdrawn, irritable, or argumentative, unable to take customary care of their appearance, frequently complaining of aches and pains, or expressing concerns of illness. We also need to ensure that licensure practices are nondiscriminatory and require disclosure of misconduct, malpractice, or impaired professional abilities, rather than just a diagnosis, mental or physical. We need to educate physicians, state licensing boards, hospitals, and insurers about the public health benefits of encouraging physicians to seek treatment for depression and suicidality.

We must also systematically inform medical students about the stressors they will be exposed to later in their practice, have open discussions of the stress encountered in a medical career, encourage better self-care, stay connected with support systems, and have provision of discreet and confidential access to psychotherapy. The culture of medicine accords low priority to physician mental health, despite evidence of untreated mood disorders and an increased burden of suicide.

As barriers are removed and physicians confront depression and suicidality in themselves, we'll be more likely to recognize and treat these conditions in patients, including colleagues and medical students. If we can't heal ourselves, at least we can learn to recognize the need for assistance. The American Foundation for Suicide Prevention has created a website to inform physicians about diagnosing depression in themselves and their legal rights in psychiatric treatment that can be found at www.afsp.org/physician.

THE RE-AWAKENING OF MY DESIRE TO HELP

After presenting the above information at grand rounds as a second year resident, I gave the same presentation at the Society of Teachers of Family Medicine's annual meeting. After that, I rarely spoke on suicide and depression publicly again, only sharing it with a select few whom I felt would benefit from my experience. Perhaps it was the rigors of establishing and running a solo family medicine practice with disappearing profit margins that kept me quiet. But truth be told, I didn't want to become known as "the depressed physician" before I had established a reputation.

In 2017, while scrolling through Facebook, I came across a post by Dr. Pamela Wible, stating that a second year medical student had died by suicide in February 2017. What stopped me wasn't just the title, it was the picture: A young man in a white coat standing in front of a red background. "That background seems familiar," I thought. I clicked on the post and instantly a cold chill came over me as I realized that the red background was indeed familiar. It was the same background where countless numbers of my own Florida State University medical students had stood before, smiles full of hope, promise, expectation...and naivety. We had lost one of our own. I stared into his eyes as mine filled with tears. I didn't know him personally but I knew his struggle was real, as during my second year of med school I had an episode of major depression. Staring at the picture of that young man, his eyes now dimmed by death, I fired off a quick email to the dean of the Daytona Beach Florida State University College of Medicine. I asked if I could come and share my story with his students. I'm naturally more of an introvert, but my silence wasn't saving anyone. Dr. Dunn promptly agreed. My "presentation" was nothing fancy—no animated slides, just a depression inventory and me sitting on a stool being transparent about my challenges with my soon-to-be colleagues. At the students' request, I returned the following year to speak again. I also shared what I know now about maintaining optimal physical, mental, and spiritual health. Every year, we lose what is the equivalent of an entire medical school to suicide, depriving more than one million Americans of their trusted, wonderful physicians. I'm on a mission to change that. We must do a better job of detecting depression and making sure those of us who are depressed have access to treatment.

8

DR. DELICIA'S SENSUAL THERAPEUTIC APPROACH

In my clinic I write several different types of prescriptions every day. Oftentimes, I write a prescription medication to assist patients who are severely depressed. There is no shame in taking a pill to treat depression, and we should recognize that it is not the only way to support your mood. No one has a monopoly on health, and healing does not happen in a vacuum. Everything around you can play a role to optimize or be an obstacle to your health. There are multiple causes of depression, so treatment needs to be multi-modal. I believe in taking an integrative and holistic approach. While my expertise is in family medicine, in addition to my own training, I draw on the expertise of several other health professionals. I recommend engaging all your senses in lifting and maintaining your mood. Several of my patients with whom I take this integrative and holistic approach call it "Dr. Delicia's Sensual Treatment of Depression." It's true in the sense that I really do integrate all five senses, both in treatment and more importantly, in the maintenance phase. My approach is holistic in that it appeals to mental, physical, and spiritual treatments, and is integrative because it draws from several healing modalities. Once anyone has ever had an issue with mental health, we know that it can be a chronic condition and not something that you treat just once. It is vitally important that you monitor your mood and intervene if it continues to decline. I help my patients create a joy box that appeals to each sense. By itself, this is not sufficient to treat severe depressive symptoms, but stopping the decline is the first step toward improving your mood.

When most people think of the sense of touch, they think of things they can feel. Silk against your skin; toes in the grass; cuddling fur babies; submerging your body in a tub full of warm water. Human touch is powerful. I have a massage therapist, Jerry Daniels, for whom I am very thankful. No matter how stressed I feel, I have never made it through a massage session without falling asleep.

Touch also relates to our social circles and the importance of connection and staying in touch with other people. No man or woman is an island. Several of the risk factors for suicide and depression include disrupted relationships. Healthy relationships are vital to your mental health. When struggling with depression, it is crucial to have a support system, a friend you can get in touch with at 2 a.m., someone you can be completely vulnerable with, who will love you anyway. Matt Gill and Lisa Nichols refer to these people as those who will love you through your ugly. Love only becomes unconditional when it is tested by conditions. Pay attention to the people who stay with you when times are tough. Who is going to be there for you when you're walking through fire or when you feel like you're drowning? Those are your true friends. Stay in touch with the people who bring you joy and uplift you, as depression often leads to isolation. I remember thinking I didn't want to take anyone else down with me. Remember to avoid isolation. Get connected and stay connected to the people that bring out your best self.

Just as important, recognize that there are some people you need to love from a distance. It doesn't mean that you don't love them, they just can't be in your inner circle at that time, maybe never, and that's ok. Pay attention to how the people around you influence your mood. Obviously, who you choose as a partner in life is extremely important, but when you are single, you should be especially discerning about the people you choose in your day-to-day walk. This may mean you need to practice loving toxic people from a distance. This may mean letting go of some dramatic friends, or people who mean well but with whom you feel your energy level dropping when they are around.

It is also important that you stay connected to your source. I am a Christian. I know that word carries A LOT of baggage (some of my most demoralizing experiences have occurred in religious environments), but my relationship to God has seen me through, time and time again. Find your source, something bigger than you, and stay connected to it.

When I think back to how I used to respond to stressors, I would go into my shell and try to work my way out of it without asking for help. Like many Black professional women, being anything other than strong all the time was not an option. I've learned that asking for help is not weakness. One of the one of the most beautiful experiences you can create for someone else is a space where they can be vulnerable with you and you can be vulnerable with them about what you need. Your friends really do want to be there for you. Friendship was made for adversity and adversity is part of life.

Touch Exercise: *Make a list of items that feel good to the touch. This may be a handkerchief, a button, anything you get tactile pleasure from touching. You can have more than one, but choose at least one. Next, place these items so they are always near you. If you are creating your own "joy box" place it there. Other places to consider include your desk, your bag, your locker or in your car. I have an embroidered satin handkerchief at my desk. When my staff sees me sitting in deep thought, sliding it through my fingers, they usually decide to come back later.*

_____

_____

_____

_____

_____

_____

_____

_____

_____

_____

_____

_____

Touch Exercise: *Make a list of the people you spend the most time with and how you feel in their presence. Do they bring you joy or pain and frustration? Is there someone you need to love from a distance?*

_____

_____

_____

_____

_____

_____

_____

_____

_____

_____

_____

_____

_____

_____

_____

TASTE

The next sense we'll explore is one I enjoy indulging. Taste is one of my favorite senses, but it can easily get you in trouble. Under the influence of depression, the palate will crave quick energy sources, also known as comfort food. No one ever craved celery when they were stressed. Pizza, chips, ice cream, wine—now that's a different story. We tend to reach for simple carbohydrates, a quick energy supply for that "fight or flight" response.

When you're trying to maintain your mood, be sure to fuel your body with food that is both delicious and nutritious, like vegetables, omega-3, and high quality protein. Eat when you're hungry, not bored. Over eating and under eating are both symptoms of depression, so get to know your pattern. When I'm feeling down and there are golden arches within a mile of me, next thing I know I'm in the drive-through line for fries and a milkshake (and I know better)! When I'm feeling stressed, I actively avoid certain driving routes because they are lined with tempting comfort food. Pat yourself on the back every time you make a good choice, and forgive yourself and make a better plan when you fall off the wagon.

Charles Stanley, a preacher I listened to online throughout med school, used the acronym HALT, and instructed to never let yourself get too **H**ungry, too **A**ngry, too **L**onely, or too **T**ired. Emotional eating is especially challenging. When was the last time you needed a hug and ordered a milkshake? When I'm about to make a decision, I try to make sure that I'm not in the extremes of hunger, anger, loneliness, or tiredness. We tend to make our worst decisions during those times. When it comes to depression, keep in mind that environment is really important. What do you have around you? What nutrition do you have quick access to? I have to make sure that there are no Reese's cups or Haribo gummy bears around me when my mood is getting low, because I know those are my kryptonite. Look around your house and make sure that you don't have foods that are going to derail your efforts. This is especially true if you tend to reach for alcohol or other substances. As my surgical colleagues say, when in doubt, cut it out.

Emotional eating is a challenge, but really making sure that your environment is helping you goes a long way. I go down to Kale Café, a Jamaican inspired vegan restaurant in Daytona Beach multiple times a week. I've found that a diet with high quality protein has helped me improve my mood considerably, but Kale Café serves really tasty food and lots of vegetables, so I can indulge my taste buds while maintaining my health. I believe in enjoying your calories and choosing foods that are really nutritious. At one of my first wine tasting experiences, I sat on a bench with a guy who was a professional sommelier. He was the epitome of an annoying dinner guest. He was swirling, sipping, rolling, splashing and spiting cabernet everywhere, even on me! But what I found impressive was that his palate was so refined, he was able to state where in the world the grape was from and whether or not the soil was acidic. He even guessed from which side of the mountain the grape was harvested. Now, this may have all been an elaborate hoax to annoy me, but he was right. Every. Single. Time. It made me think about how I eat. When we're eating, how often do we really let the food break down in our mouth and interact with all of our taste buds—the sweet taste on the tip of your tongue, the sour taste on the sides of the tongue, and for all those black coffee lovers, picking up that bitter taste on the back of the tongue? How often do you eat something and take the time to pick out the influences of subtle nutmeg or clove, or really enjoy the oral phase of eating versus just gobbling? It takes about 20 minutes for the messages from your gut to tell your brain that you are full. In that time, if you're absentmindedly reaching with your snack hand, you could have put down a lot of calories that you didn't even enjoy having. By the time those messages reach your brain, you've likely over eaten and are headed into a sugar crash or food coma. Take time to enjoy and savor every bite.

Nutrition is important for your mood. The building blocks of neurotransmitters are amino acids. Some individuals notice an improvement in their mood by taking the approach of focusing on supporting their nutritional foundation. L-tyryptophan, tyrosine, and 5HTP are all amino acids that by increasing their intake, some individuals have found improved moods. Eating a diet rich in good fats like omega-3, high quality protein, and vegetables is widely accepted for general health. Anti-inflammatory diets like the Mediterranean diet are very healthful. Likewise, avoiding simple carbohydrates, sweets, and highly processed foods is equally effective. Choose your fuel wisely. Check out my friend Dr. Lauren Powell, the Culinary Doctor for more tips on using food as delicious medicine.

"My body will live out my life's purpose.
I feed it accordingly."

~ Lisa Nichols

Taste Exercise: *Cleanse the cupboards and refine the refrigerator. Take a moment to look at the food items you have readily available. Are they good fats like avocado or high in omega-3s like salmon? Are your cupboards loaded with cookies, candies, white bread, and processed foods? Take the first steps to creating an environment of success. Toss out those processed, simple carbohydrate, junk foods. Throwing them away will cost you less in the long run than keeping them around.*

SIGHT

Positive visualization is one of most important tools athletes and peak performers use to create success. Jack Canfield teaches the importance of affirmations, visualization, emotionalization, consistent repetition, and inspired action in his book *The Success Principles*. The sense of sight is very influential. You can never un-see anything, so sight can be the source of intense trauma or of extreme pleasure. When was the last time you stood in awe, absorbing a breathtaking view? There is beauty all around us but depression slowly robs us of the ability to experience it. There are certain images that make you smile simply by looking at them.

For me, it is the image of water. Every time I take a bridge over the Intracoastal Waterway and see the expanse of ocean water, I'm reminded why I live in Daytona Beach. I also love coming home to a clean organized home, so I gladly pay someone to help me maintain it. I have pictures of my loved ones around my home and office. Looking at them keeps me in tune to what really matters. I maintain an environment that I find inviting and that I am excited to see. In my office I have pictures of my parents because they are two amazing individuals. They love me unconditionally. They're proud that I'm a doctor, but they would have been proud no matter what I decided to do. I have days when things don't seem to be working out and it's nice to be around people who love me and don't want anything from me, even if they are just there in picture form. Certain images have a way of almost transporting you to a simpler time. I have a Polaroid picture of my father and I circa 2002 at a Christmas party. We went not realizing that we were supposed to come with a talent to perform. We were wondering what to do and my dad started hamboning. He went to town slapping his knees, my knees, his chest, and stomping and I joined in tapping my foot with syncopated clapping. We had the absolute best time and it was truly spontaneous. No matter what I'm going through, when I look at that picture, I am taken back to that moment and the complete joy I experienced creating music with my dad. That moment is always available to me when I need a pick-me-up and I keep that picture in my visual field.

Sight Exercise: *Think about the landscapes, people, and visuals that spontaneously make you smile. Take a picture of them and keep it in sight. Set it as your screen saver or frame it. This is especially important when you need extra motivation to do what you have to do so you can do what you want to do. Depression is often like walking around with dark glasses and blinders. It's important to keep the bigger picture in sight and mind.*

_____

_____

_____

_____

_____

_____

_____

_____

_____

_____

_____

_____

SMELL

Have you ever walked into a restaurant and a familiar aroma makes you grin? One of my favorite items in my joy box indulges my sense of smell. Why? Because it goes straight to the brainstem. You don't have to think or reason about it. There are certain smells that instantly take you back to beautiful childhood memories. The smell of corn reminds me of being at my grandmother's house making hot water corn-bread. The smell of cherry Chapstick takes me back to being on the school bus in third grade, a time when I felt like a queen. I keep cherry Chapstick in my office, car, and home. All of us have certain smells that remind us of beautiful times in our childhood or life. I love that there is such an interest around aroma therapy, and the attributes and properties of particular aromas. Here, I am specifically referring to the personal associations you have with certain smells. Smells can instantly make you feel a little bit better if it's something that reminds you of a happy experience. The first part of treating depression is stopping the decline, and a smell with a strong emotional connection to a positive experience can be a powerful mood pick me up.

When a fragrance is inhaled, the airborne odor molecule travels up the nostrils to the olfactory epithelium. Olfactory receptor cells are triggered and send an impulse to the olfactory bulb. Each olfactory receptor type sends an impulse to a particular microregion, or glomerulus, of the olfactory bulb. There are around

2,000 glomeruli in the olfactory bulb, which receive the impulses from the olfactory receptors and allows us to perceive many smells. The olfactory bulb then transmits the impulses to other parts of the brain, including the gustatory center (where the sensation of taste is perceived), the amygdala (where emotional memories are stored), and other parts of the limbic system.

Because the limbic system is directly connected to those parts of the brain that control heart rate, blood pressure, breathing, memory, stress levels, and hormone balance, essential oils can have profound physiological and psychological effects.[x]

Essential Oils pocket reference, Life Science Publishing; 6th edition (2014)

The sense of smell is the only one of the five senses so directly linked to the limbic lobe of the brain. The emotional control center—anxiety, depression, fear, anger, and joy—all emanate from this region. The scent of a special fragrance can evoke memories and emotions before we are even consciously aware of it. When smells are concerned, we react first and think later. All of the other senses—touch, taste, hearing and sight—are routed through the thalamus, which acts as the switchboard for the brain passing stimuli on to the cerebral cortex, the conscious thought center, and other parts of the brain.

The limbic lobe, a group of brain structures that includes the hippocampus and amygdala located below the cerebral cortex, can also directly activate the hypothalamus. The hypothalamus is one of the most important parts of the brain. It controls body temperature, hunger, thirst, fatigue, sleep and circadian cycles. It acts as our hormonal control center and releases hormones that can affect many functions of the body. The production of growth hormones, sex hormones, thyroid hormones, and neurotransmitters such as serotonin are all governed by the hypothalamus. Fragrance can directly stimulate the limbic lobe and the hypothalamus, which is responsive to olfactory stimuli. This treatment may not be effective for someone who has lost their sense of smell, but if your olfaction is intact, fragrance can be a powerful mood lifter to help treat and prevent depression.

Smell Exercise: *Close your eyes and imagine some of the most joyous occasions of your life and remember the smell that was associated with them. The smells of pine trees and honeysuckle take me back to my childhood days spent in Charlottesville, Virginia. For you, it may be a loved one's favorite fragrance or a freshly baked pie. Next, try to capture that smell. Find a candle, cologne, or item that you can put in your joy box or keep with you for when you need a quick mood elevator. Write about the smell that makes you smile below.*

_____

_____

_____

_____

_____

_____

_____

_____

_____

_____

_____

_____

HEARING

Now hearing, is perhaps the most important sense to target when attempting to maintain your mood. When you're experiencing depression, your self-talk is negative and filled with guilt, doubt, shame, and "should." The word "should" is not helpful and is an energetic curse word for your mood. Saying "I should feel more grateful," does nothing but lead to guilt about the lack of gratitude. Telling someone they "should be more helpful" does nothing but create the sentiment that they are not enough. My advice, avoid using should.

Don't should on others, don't let others should on you, and please don't should on yourself!

"Shoulding" may lead some people to isolate themselves. The worst thing a person dealing with depression can do is be isolated with their depressed thoughts, because the hardest part about treating depression is that you can't always trust your own mind. In depression, negative self-talk is a megaphone, while your positive self-talk becomes an unintelligible whisper. You've got to turn up the positive volume. Matt Gil who works with Lisa Nichols and Motivating the Teen Spirit used the visual of an over the shoulder hip hop beat box with controls for either speaker to demonstrate this during a retreat at Rancho La Puerta. He emphasized the need to turn down the negative side and turn up the powerful. He would often say, "Press pause on the negative and press play on the powerful." This takes practice. In the beginning it's challenging to hear the positive in your own voice, so recruiting outside help is useful.

Borrow some daily affirmations and place them on your mirror, fridge, door, etc. To be effective, they must be stated in the positive: "I am positive" vs. "I don't say negative things." Then make a daily habit of saying them out loud. I have sticky notes on my mirror and front door with affirmations such as

- "I give myself permission to fail, so I can give myself permission to fly." – Lisa Nichols

- "I have everything I need to win right now." – Dr. Kristamarie Collman

- I am ready for the world; is the world ready for me?

- I am in the right place at the right time.

- "I am more committed to my purpose than my plan." – Lisa Nichols

- I am joy. I am love. I am enough.

Jack Canfield has a CD series that I listened to several years ago called *Self-Esteem and Peak Performance*. Side 9 was completely comprised of positive affirmations, and I drove around with it every day, repeating statements like "Everything good in me increases and multiplies."

Hearing Exercise: *Choose a few of your own positive affirmations. Place them on post-it notes on your bathroom mirror, front door, refrigerator, or wherever you could use some extra support. Consider taking a picture of them and posting in our Facebook group, The Day breakers Society. Write them below.*

_____

_____

_____

_____

_____

_____

_____

_____

_____

_____

_____

_____

_____

_____

Music is great medicine. There are certain songs you can't help but bop to and feel just a smidge better, even in your darkest days. Keep those on your play list. I have a song that gets me up in the morning. It's called "Get Up" by Mary Mary and I have it set as an alarm. The line in that song, "What are you afraid of? Don't you know what you're made of; one of God's greatest creations, take this invitation and get up", always connects me to my source, my purpose, and shepherds me into the day. As a 2nd year medical student trudging through the snow up Transcript Avenue toward the University of Kentucky College of Medicine, I would sing "I don't feel no ways tired, I've come to far from where I've started from. Nobody told me the road would be easy and I don't believe He brought me this far to leave me."

What's on your mood elevation play list? When my niece Jada was 10, Will.i.am came out with "I Like to Move It," She and I would jump around dancing, singing, and shaking everything. That song reminds me of joyous times with her and makes me want to move it! Des-ree's hit "You Gotta Be" is one of my all-time favorite songs for staying grounded. And in the evenings, I like to chill to beats like "Don't You Forget It," by Glenn Lewis. Music has an amazing ability to influence mood. Use it to help elevate your mood when you need it, or to wind down and relax. Music from the baroque period has a tempo slightly above heart rate and often is beneficial as background study music.

Hearing Exercise: Everyone can benefit from a soundtrack. Take a moment to curate your go-to songs to improve your mood. Share your go to tunes in our Facebook group, The Day breakers Society, and write them below.

_____

_____

_____

_____

_____

_____

_____

_____

_____

_____

_____

_____

_____

_____

9

OVERCOME STRESS AND DEPRESSION

DAILY HABITS TO CREATE A WELL-MANAGED MIND

What is stress? Stress is the body's response to any physical or emotional changes in life. Some think of it as a trigger for our sympathetic fight, flight, or freeze response (a necessary and helpful reaction for existence). During periods of stress, you experience an elevated heart rate, which increases blood flow to muscles for running and dilates pupils for sight, all meant to protect you from harm. Today, many of our stressors are mental instead of physical, but the reaction is the same. When you're experiencing stress it's time to get active and move to use that energy. It's not time to go to sleep or self-medicate, and this includes the use of alcohol.

Our minds are powerful. To demonstrate that I'd like you to participate in a brief exercise. Think back to a specific incidence in your life that was extremely stressful.

Now think of the earliest time in your life when you experienced a similar stress. How old were you? What did you hear? See? Smell? Close your eyes and really go back to that moment as if you were back there right now. Stay there for another minute and feel what emotions come up within you. Really be there. Then, open your eyes.

Did anything change in your body? Is your heart pounding a little harder? Is your mouth dry? Do you feel ready to run or fight? Although your body was sitting safely in your chair, far away from the danger of the stressful situation you just imagined, your nervous system was preparing you for the sympathetic fight, flight, or freeze response that occurs when you are experiencing stress. This is because our brain does not know the difference between a real physical stressor and one that is in our mind. Stress affects every part of our body. Symptoms may include headache, pain, fatigue, poor concentration, errors in decision making, constriction of blood vessels, and an increased risk of heart attacks. The most common time for ER admissions due to chest pains is Monday morning when people are stressed about their return to work.

Now that you've relived that stress, it's important to dissipate it. Physical activity is a great way to relieve stress. Kendall Summerhawk employed a method that involved imagery and movement. Pretend that stress is a large six-foot ball. Extend both arms as wide as possible and try to wrap your arms around it and compact it. Compress it to the size of a beach ball. Engage your biceps, rhomboids, and core. Next, compress it down to the size of a tennis ball. Then, put that stress ball in one hand and keep pressing and packing it down with all the muscles in your hands working it down to the size of a pea. Hold the pea in the palm of your open hand. Now, simply blow it away. We must learn to shrink our stress down to size, exhale, and get rid of it.

$S = P > R$

Stress occurs when the pressure is greater than the resources, so to combat it we can either find ways of decreasing the pressure or increasing our coping resources. I employ both. Decrease the pressure and increase the resources.

STRESS LESS: 30 WAYS IN 30 PLUS DAYS

The following are some suggestions to help decrease stress. Under the cloak of depression, our to-do list must be minimized. Do not attempt to do all of them at once. Skim the list and choose the ones you feel would be most beneficial to you.

1. Be aware of your environment. Limit your chances to be exposed to a stressor. Some stressful situations are unavoidable, but often there are stressors we can anticipate and avoid. Examine your day and your surroundings. What can you put in place as a stress buffer?

2. Know your triggers. For example, when my friends are late it annoys me, so I purposely give them an early start time. Pay attention to the people and things that get under your skin. Track them in a journal.

3. Love toxic people from a distance. When people show you their true colors, believe them. Not everyone needs a front row seat in your life.

4. Learn your love language by reading Gary Chapman's book *The 5 Love Languages*." Know yours and those of the people closest to you for more harmonious personal and business unions. Because I know my own love language I can better support myself. I have my entire team take it so I know how they interpret support and how best to incentivize them.

5. Be assertive. In a retreat, my friend Margaret Packer taught us to stand up for our rights, express our thoughts, and have solid boundaries. Remember that we teach people how to treat us (even when you are an intern). Negotiate from positions of empowerment and refuse to be a victim. If your schedule, work environment, pay, etc. are not what you want, make the case for why your contribution merits improving that area.

6. Organize your day for success. Your day begins the night before. Review next day agendas. Decrease the activation energy required to start important tasks by having

everything already at hand. This helps to reduce poor decision making due to stress. Proper organization makes you less reliant on memorization. Consider what steps you can take to better prepare and organize for the next day.

Share the professional organizer or technology you've found helpful in the Day breakers Society Facebook page.

7. Automate everything. What can you automate or create a system around to decrease the amount of time you personally invest? At home or at work, having a clear system for things ensures they will get done.

    "Systems liberate you." ~ Kendall Summerhawk.

8. Create rituals that help you. For example, disconnect from work every day by clearing your desk, and driving home listening to relaxing music. It helps you leave work at work and mentally shift gears. In the morning before I allow my feet to touch the floor, I start my day listening to my favorite song and meditating on my favorite scriptures:

    "The fruit of the spirit is love, joy, peace, patience, kindness, goodness, faithfulness, gentleness, and self-control. Against these things there is no law" Galatians 5:22-23 (KJV).

    "**God has** not **given us the spirit** of fear, but **of power and of love and of a sound mind**" II Timothy 2:15 (NKJV).

"...be transformed by the renewing of your mind" Romans 12:2 (KJV).

Examine your morning routine, what tweaks would help you start your day more relaxed?

_____

_____

_____

_____

_____

_____

_____

_____

_____

_____

_____

_____

_____

_____

9. Get 8 hours of uninterrupted sleep each night. Don't sleep on sleep. Keep a soothing, quiet, cool, dark environment reserved only for sleep and sex. Sleep deprivation sets us up for emotional instability and fatigue.

10. Celebrate every step. Do this especially when you're going after your goals and still dealing with depressive symptoms. Recognize that your pace will need to change and your to-do list of thirty actions may need to become three. If you get one thing done, celebrate that one thing. Every step in the right direction is a step in the right direction. What can you celebrate today?

_____

_____

_____

_____

_____

_____

_____

_____

_____

11. Identify your goals. What is your WHY? Set short and long term goals. What would you like to experience this moment, day, week, month, year, decade? They are all related. Understand what drives you. Only you know what you really want.

    Exercise: write ONE goal for each time period and make a positive affirmation for each goal.

    Day _____

    _____

    Week _____

    _____

    Month _____

    _____

    Year _____

    _____

    Decade _____

    _____

12. Set S.M.A.R.T., measurable goals. What do you want to accomplish and by when? What is measured gets done. How will you know you've succeeded if there is no pre-

determined goal? (Smart goals are Specific, Measurable, Assignable, Realistic, and Time-Based):

Exercise: Make S.M.A.R.T list:

S. _____

_____

M. _____

_____

A. _____

_____

R. _____

_____

T. _____

_____

13. Reverse engineer your goals. Busy isn't purposeful. Your purpose is too precious to be hijacked by busywork. Prioritize your goals by dividing things into a list of must, should, and like. Do what matters most. Focus on what you must do so you can do what you like to do. Consider letting go of the "shoulds."

14. Learn to delegate like a pro. Engage your team and community to help. Teamwork makes the dream work. Ask yourself if the task is the highest use of your skills and gifts. If not, give it to someone who would be a better fit.

    "Let yourself be silently drawn by the stronger pull of what you really love."- Rumi

15. Feel the fear and do it anyway. It's both the title of a good book and a way to approach life. Fear is the only thing that gets smaller as you walk toward it. A pastor mentioned once that FEAR stands for False Evidence Appearing Real. Your love has to be greater than your fear. Life begins on the edge of your comfort zone and the more you stretch your comfort zone, the wider it gets. I used to get vasovagal and almost faint at the thought of public speaking. Now I speak to thousands and enjoy sharing. Don't let fear hijack your purpose.

16. Take inventory of your day. Looking at the way we spend our time is eye opening. Recognize and minimize distractions, whether it's turning off notifications on your phone or limiting screen time. Social media has its benefits and many, many detractions. It keeps us in comparison with someone else's heavily curated and filtered life. Identify and avoid time wasters. Avoid aimlessly flipping through catalogues. Click bait can wait.

Exercise: Take inventory of how you spend the next 24 hours.

_____

_____

_____

_____

_____

_____

_____

_____

_____

_____

_____

_____

_____

_____

_____

17. Turn your to-do list into a calendar with adequate buffer time. Give everything you want to experience or get done a specific day and time, especially the fun stuff!

18. Say no. It's enticing to overcommit, but in order to say yes to the things you really want, you'll have to say no more often. Having too much on your plate and feeling like you're not getting things done can be demoralizing. Consider giving these opportunities to other people who would be happy to do them.

19. Give your goals titillating titles. My coach, Lisa Nichols, had an amazing physical transformation that followed her internal transformation. She found the word "exercising" to be less palatable so she put "snatching my sexy back" on her calendar to motivate her to keep to a nutrition and fitness routine. The results speak for themselves. Change your perception, change your reality.

20. Focus. Multi-tasking is a myth. Do. One. Thing. At. A. Time. When people text and drive, they are no longer driving, they're just texting at a dangerous rate of speed. Be fully present and you'll get more done. Being busy is not the same as being productive.

21. Separate the occurrence of events from their meaning. Challenge how you think about the stressor. An event only has the meaning you give it. While at Awesomeness Fest in 2015, there was a presentation illustrating the importance

of separating events from their meaning. It was even more powerful because Marty, the presenter, used his own cancer diagnosis as an event that only had the meaning he chose to give it. He may have had cancer, but cancer didn't have him. Often, events and meanings are formed early on in childhood and become so entwined that it becomes difficult to separate the two. Left unchecked, similar events will go on to trigger meanings for the rest of your life. The best way to decrease the association of an event to the meaning you've given it is to entertain an alternate meaning. Just the fact that there is another explanation or possible meaning out there automatically loosens the grasp of the earlier association. For example, after a break up (event), you may be triggered by past experiences to think that you're not good enough. An alternate meaning could be that now you're single and ready to meet the partner you wanted all along.

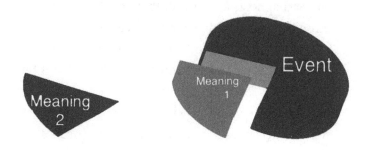

Exercise: List some events you perceive as negative and the meanings you gave them. Then list some alternate meanings those events could have.

_____

_____

_____

_____

_____

_____

_____

22. Employ thought stopping techniques. Press delete on negative thoughts. In the moment, you don't have time to thoughtfully unravel the meaning your 7-year-old self gave an event. A quick physical thing you can do to interrupt negative thoughts is to physically press on a hard object as if you're hitting the delete button on your keyboard.

23. Daily affirmations. Begin and end each day with gratitude and grace. Begin a meditation or mindfulness practice, which is an essential workout for your head. It only takes 10 to 20 minutes each morning to adopt a practice. Mindful meditation is very beneficial according to Dr. Varma, who says "We find that there are actual changes in the brain. Real structural changes. Gray matter has increased. Your amygdala, which is the fear center of the brain, shrinks. Your hippocampus increases in size from learning. The hippocampus is a part of the brain involved in learning and memory so meditation mindfulness has shown really powerful changes in the brain."[xi]

24. Get physical. Exercise, especially in the morning. Your morning sets the tone for your day. Exercise releases endorphins, your natural mood lifters. Dr. Carol Penn's "Movement Is My Medicine" approach offers some helpful resources.

25. Laugh. Tickle me Tuesday belly shaking laughs improve breathing and muscle tension.

26. Accept support. Givers aren't always good at receiving. Sometimes we turn down the very help we need because we want to handle things on our own. Let good people help you.

27. Create community. No man is an island. Join a group of masterminds working toward similar goals. Create space where you can be both vulnerable and a super hero. We were meant to live in interconnectedness. Social isolation is rampant. Nourish authentic empowering relationships.

28. "Say yes to yourself no matter what." ~ Kailash

29. Fill your cup. "Serve from your overflow." ~ Lisa Nichols.

Take time to recharge. Imagine a tea cup sitting on a saucer. The tea cup is you. Fill your life with exciting things that feed your passion, like music, pleasant aromas, biking, boating, hiking, or gardening. You have to fill yourself up with the things that bring you joy. Pour it in until your cup is overflowing. What's in the cup is for you! When you serve others, serve them from your overflow. We take care of what we value. Take care of yourself. It's why every airline says "Put the oxygen on yourself first before you assist others."

30. Say "I love you" to yourself. Write three things you love and respect about yourself.

    1. _____

    2. _____

    3. _____

There is nothing selfish about taking care of yourself.

10

COMPLETION NOT PERFECTION: TAKE IMPERFECT ACTION

If comparison is the thief of all joy, perfectionism will rob you of ever getting your to-dos done. My coach, Dr. Draion Burch, encourages imperfect action. Stay in action, because even the seemingly small actions add up and build momentum. Momentum will help you break through barriers so you can achieve your dreams. Imagine the momentum of a downhill stream of water. I love water. It's one of the reasons I live in coastal Florida. I love feeling it flow through my hands and over my body. Water is always changing and change is inevitable and necessary. Water is strong, cohesive, moves objects or flows around them, gradually shaping their surface. Sometimes we have to be flexible en route to our destination. Be like water. Keep moving. As Joan Baez said, "Action is the antidote to despair."

Ask the right question. For example, you could ask "Why am I so ____?" Positive or negative, whatever you put in the blank, your brain will go through its file cabinet of memories to pull out ones to support that statement. Your subconscious mind believes what you tell it. For example, if you ask "Why did this happen to me?" according to my friend, Sean Smith of Pink Caddie Coaching, the answer to that question will define you.

My friend Dr. Lauren often says, "It's always a story with you." I'm not a dramatic person, but in navigating, negotiating, and operating as a single business owner, I've had more than my fair share of drama over the years. After describing one of my eventful days, Dr. Lauren said, "This happens to you because you can handle it." She is right. And just as I have survived obstacles in my life, you have survived everything that you've been through. All of it, good and bad, shapes who you are. Your current test will someday be your testimony. You don't get the testimony without the test.

Your experiences are not just about you. Ultimately, I'm a better physician because I've struggled with depression. It stays at the top of mind and causes me to give depression surveys with the same regularity as blood glucose and blood pressure diaries. Keeping track of mental health is important. If you don't measure it, you can't manage it.

Life is full of distractions. It's easy to be busy doing things that don't advance us to our desired goal. Often, people who have successfully climbed the corporate ladder get to the top and realize their ladder was leaning against the wrong building, but even then, it's never too late to change. This is especially true of physicians. We spend years in training, believing someday it will all be worth it. Then some of us graduate and start practicing in environments where we are forced to see patients like cattle, with no time to really connect, educate, and care.

It's never too late to build a better life. I started my solo family medicine practice straight out of residency and unintentionally built my own prison. In 2015, I switched to a direct primary care business model that supported the vision I had when I entered medical school. Sometimes it's not what you're doing, but how you are doing it that is the problem. I knew I was meant to be a physician, but my insurance-based clinic limited how much time I was able to spend with each patient. Now I have designed a personally and professionally fulfilling practice. I help physicians who are enduring clinical medicine thrive by transitioning to direct primary care with grace and ease so they can practice medicine in line with their vision and values.

Stay authentic to what works for you and keep your victories visible. This advice is best illustrated in one of my favorite bible stories. Out of all the biblical lessons, the story of Daniel and Goliath is one I draw so many lessons from that help in overcoming depression. You don't have to be religious-minded to get value from it and I'll bottom line it for you. Daniel was a shepherd. It was his job to look after the sheep and defend them from predators. He killed lions and bears with a sling shot. Goliath and his army came to fight against Israel and David agreed to fight him. His well-meaning friend tried to give him their armor to take into battle, but David chose to use what had worked for him all along instead of their clunky protective layers. He killed Goliath with a sling shot—cut off his head and kept Goliath's armor with him to remember his victory. Always do what works for you and keep reminders of what you've overcome in your visual field every day. My diplomas are prominently displayed in my office. It's not just for the benefit of the patients knowing my credentials. It's a reminder that whatever this day brings, I've faced and overcome obstacles before, and I'll do it again.

What situations in your past have you overcome? What items remind you of those victories?

_____

_____

_____

_____

_____

_____

_____

I was in a coaching group with Lisa Nichols shortly after transitioning the business model of Family First Health Center from insurance based to direct primary care. I knew it was the right thing to do for my own mental health and the type of medicine I wanted to provide, but not all of my patients were initially excited about the change. For many, the status quo of me being an insurance-based physician worked for them. My mental health could have been in a better place and I experienced a lot of guilt. I was talking to Lisa Nichols trying to get some advice about how to better explain to my patients the value of what I was offering. Lisa sat there and listened, then began picking at her skin. Lisa is known for her gift of language, but instead of speaking she repeated this motion for literally 20 seconds, as if she was unraveling strings. And in Lisa Nichols' world, 20 seconds is a long time. After asking the question and waiting for her to use her words, finally she said, "You know, I want you to take off the boxing gloves. I want you to stop beating yourself up." I didn't realize I was doing it until she brought it to my attention. As my coach, Dr. Bonnie Mason of Beyond the Exam Room later said, "Sometimes we need to stop giving ourselves a left hook. We actually need to take ourselves off the hook." We have to be kind to and forgive ourselves. We have to look at what's on our plate and make sure that what's on it aligns with the season that we're in.

From being an athlete for several years, I recognized that I always did my best when I had a coach, someone who was watching my form, looking at the bigger picture and giving me insight and direction. That's really what I'm doing now, working with a group of physicians who are all striving to be the best that they can be and to make a bigger impact. Transitioning the way I practice medicine allowed me to have time to focus on my passions and inspire other physicians to do the same. I've made even deeper connections to my community.

The subject of suicide and depression has been a calling for me for a really long time that I ran away from because I didn't want to be known as the depressed doctor. The other reason I was reluctant to talk about depression is because I knew I wasn't immune. One episode of major depressive disorder increases your likelihood of having a second one by 50%; two episodes increase it by 75%, and three increases the chances for a fourth episode by 90 to 95%.[xi] I thought, what if I start speaking about this and then I have another episode? But the truth is, as Anthony Trucks explains, "Our vulnerability protects us."

There are a lot of things that I do daily to maintain my mental health. I've been able to share with my patients and I look forward to sharing it with more people. As physicians and physicians-in- training, we become very good at being there for everyone else, but we are not as good at taking care of ourselves and making sure that our health is a priority. We have to heal ourselves. I love treating depression because I love helping people reach their full potential. The cloak of depression prevents your unique awesomeness from shining through. When we peel depression away, we have the opportunity of being our authentic self. Understanding depression provides a key to experiencing happiness. A disease does not define you.

I've gone from silence to sharing my "Dying on the Vine: Overcoming Depression and Suicide Amongst Physicians" talk around the globe. By openly discussing the incidence of depression and making physician wellbeing a priority, we won't have to stare into the eyes of our departed colleagues. In the words of one of my mentors, Lisa Nichols, "Fill YOUR cup first. SERVE from your OVERFLOW." So I reach out to you today as colleagues, peers, and friends: Rather than shriveling on the vine in the service of others, let's thrive on the vine together. The journey of a thousand steps starts with a made up mind. Decide today to make self-care a priority.

I am forever thankful to the distraction of my family pet and to my high school English teacher Mrs. Bowker who intervened during those dark winter high school days when I almost took fistfuls of pills to end my pain. There is a thin line between suicidal ideation and action. Many suicide attempt survivors say the suicidal act, although planned, was impulsive. Several survivors instantly regretted their attempt. Later they ask, "What was I thinking?"

Truth is, they weren't thinking, the depression was. You do not have to believe, act on, or listen to every thought you have. I know I am fortunate to have had family, friends, spiritual leaders, and administrators looking out for me when I experienced a second episode of depression in medical school. With more than half of today's physicians experiencing "burnout" and approximately one third experiencing depression, it is past time to intervene.

My silence will not save anyone, but sharing my story can, and so can yours. If you are in need of a speaker to educate, inspire, and motivate your team, it would be my honor.

It is my hope that by sharing my story and these prevention strategies, I can shine a light for medical students and physicians in their darkest hours to help them overcome stress and depression, so they can show up and share their amazing gifts with the world—but first, heal themselves.

For more information on Physician Well Being, contact the American Foundation for Suicide Prevention @ www.afsp.org

If you're feeling suicidal or just need to talk, call the National Suicide Prevention Lifeline for free at 1-800-273-8255.

Here are a few online directories to help find a therapist in your area:

- PsychCentral:
  www.psychcentral.com/find-help

- Psychology Today:
  www.therapists.psychologytoday.com/rms

- GoodTherapy.org:
  www.goodtherapy.org/find-therapist.html

SOURCES

1. Dawn K. Brown, MD of Dr. Dawn Psych MD

2. Diagnostic and Statistical manual of Mental Disorders, 5th Edition: DSM-5

3. OB/GYN News March 1, 2003

4. Women Physicians Health Study 1999 American Journal of Psychiatry

5. Eva Schernhammer, M.D., Dr. P.H. Taking Their Own Lives- The High rate of Physician Suicide NEngl J Med 352; 24 June 16, 2005

6. Tracy Hampton, PhD Experts Address risk of Physician Suicide Jama Sept 14, 2005- Vol 294, No.10

7. Oppenheimer K, Miller M, Forney P. Effect of history of psychological counseling on selection of applicants for residencies. J Med Educ 1987;62:504-508

8. Medical Licensure Questions Abut Mental Illness and compliance with the Americans With Disabilities Act James T.R. Jones et al Journal of the American Academy of Psychiatry and the Law December 2018, 46 (4) 458-471

9. Dr. Katherine Gold Newsy Unspoken: Doctor Depression and Suicide

10. Essential Oils pocket reference 6th edition Life Science products & publishing May 2014

11. Med Circle Interview 2018 Dr. Sue Varma

ABOUT THE AUTHOR

Dr. Delicia Haynes is a board-certified physician and the founder and CEO of Family First Health Center, an integrative membership-based family medicine clinic in Daytona Beach, Florida. She is revolutionizing America's healthcare system within the Direct Primary Care movement, transitioning her medical practice into the first DPC clinic in Volusia County in 2015.

Dr. Haynes strives to make an impact in her field, she is past president of the Volusia County Medical Society. She is also a diplomat of the American Board of Family Medicine and the American Board of Obesity Medicine. Dr. Haynes is passionate about ending the pattern of depression and suicide in the medical community. She speaks widely about the risk factors, advocating an integrative approach to treating depression. Dr. Haynes is on a mission to create a world where no one feels the need to write a suicide note and no one has to read one.

Learn more at www.drdeliciamd.com